T0413545

CANNABIS STARTUP SUCCESS

A COMPREHENSIVE GUIDE FOR NEW ENTREPRENEURS

RICH CAMPBELL

hymind Media, llc
Subsidiary of RM Campbell Acquisitions, LLC

Cannabis Startup Success: A Comprehensive
Guide for New Entrepreneurs
©Rich Campbell

Print ISBN: 979-8-89692-044-1
eBook ISBN: 979-8-89692-043-4

Cannabis Startup Success: A Comprehensive
Guide for New Entrepreneurs
©Rich Campbell

Print ISBN: 979-8-89692-044-1
eBook ISBN: 979-8-89692-043-4

CANNABIS STARTUP SUCCESS

A COMPREHENSIVE GUIDE FOR NEW ENTREPRENEURS

RICH CAMPBELL

hymind Media, llc
Subsidiary of RM Campbell Acquisitions, LLC

CONTENTS

ABOUT THE GUIDE

"Cannabis Startup Success: A Comprehensive Guide for New Entrepreneurs" is a practical and empowering guide for aspiring cannabis entrepreneurs. The book's underlying message is that with the right knowledge, tools, and mindset, anyone can successfully navigate the complexities of the cannabis industry and build a thriving business. It emphasizes the importance of staying informed about the evolving legal landscape, understanding market dynamics, and implementing best practices to ensure long-term success. The book is designed to be an accessible and comprehensive resource, providing step-by-step guidance, real-world examples, and actionable insights to help readers transform their cannabis business dreams into reality.

AUDIENCE

Aspiring cannabis entrepreneurs, existing business owners entering the cannabis market, industry professionals, investors, and students. The book offers practical guidance, comprehensive coverage, actionable insights, and industry-specific knowledge, making it essential for success in the cannabis industry.

BENEFIT

The guide offers step-by-step instructions, checklists, and real-world examples, making complex concepts easy to implement. It covers legal considerations, marketing strategies, and more, providing a well-rounded knowledge base. Each section gives actionable steps to navigate challenges and seize opportunities. It addresses the unique aspects of the cannabis industry, including regulatory compliance and market trends, making it a valuable resource.

MY CANNABIS STORY

In 2012, my life was a whirlwind of family and ambition. My sons were navigating the challenges of high school, while the youngest was just beginning his journey in elementary school. Amidst the chaos of school runs, games, and parent-teacher meetings, I stumbled upon an article in *TIME* magazine that would redefine my professional trajectory. This article wasn't just a story; it was a gateway into the nascent world of the cannabis industry, a sector ripe with potential yet labyrinthine in its legalities and regulations.

Fascinated, I began to envision a future in this emerging field. The next few years were a blend of family commitments and professional exploration. I spent countless hours researching the cannabis industry, balancing my time between the boys' school/sports activities. The challenge was to find a way into this industry that was still in its infancy yet growing rapidly.

The turning point came in 2018. During one of my regular visits to my oldest son's NFL pro day training, I reconnected with his former high school basketball coach, who had transitioned into a successful career in wealth management. Our conversation over breakfast soon turned to the potential of the cannabis industry. Energized by the prospect, I set out to create a business proposal that would attract serious investment.

After a joyous and relaxing vacation interruption, I returned with a renewed focus. My friend, an ever-reliable business partner in my past ventures, joined me in this new endeavor. Together, we traveled across the country, exploring opportunities in legal states, seeking a business that embodied the full spectrum of the cannabis industry.

However, the deeper we dove, the more apparent the industry's knowledge gap became. It wasn't just about growing and selling; it was about understanding a complex and evolving landscape. This realization steered us towards technology, leading to the inception of Canoja. Our goal was to create solutions that bring clarity and transparency to the industry.

Throughout this journey, I recognized the power of shared knowledge. My experiences, from balancing family life with entrepreneurial aspirations to navigating the uncharted waters of the cannabis industry, were invaluable lessons that needed to be shared. This led to the creation of a comprehensive guide, designed not only as a recounting of my path into the cannabis industry but as a roadmap for others to follow.

This guide represents the culmination of years of learning, a balance between family life and a relentless pursuit of a dream in the cannabis industry. It's a vibrant, dynamic guide packed with essential resources, designed to empower your personal venture in this flourishing field. As a testament to the journey of a father and entrepreneur, this guide aims to inspire and guide the next wave of cannabis entrepreneurs. It's a treasure trove of insights and strategies, meticulously compiled from my experiences. This isn't just my story – it's a roadmap for your success, a beacon to navigate the intriguing, ever-changing landscape of the cannabis industry. Dive in, explore its depths, and let it be the catalyst for your own trailblazing journey. I invite you to engage with me on social media, share your thoughts, and become a part of this ever-evolving story. Let's explore the possibilities together and grow in this blossoming industry.

Your adventure starts here, and the possibilities are as limitless as your ambition!

OVERVIEW OF THE CANNABIS INDUSTRY

Changing Legal Landscape: As part of an overview of the dynamic regulatory framework, it's crucial to note the recent DEA rescheduling of cannabis to Schedule III. This decision is pivotal, signaling potential shifts in everything from federal enforcement to insurance and banking services for cannabis businesses.

The global cannabis industry has experienced a remarkable transformation in recent years, reshaping the way we perceive and utilize this once-stigmatized plant. Internationally, changing attitudes, evolving regulations, and a growing understanding of its medical and economic potential have fueled its expansion. In the United States, a patchwork of state-level legalization efforts has led to a thriving domestic market, while the industry grapples with federal prohibition. This overview provides a snapshot of the dynamic cannabis landscape, both on a global scale and within the complex regulatory framework of the United States, shedding light on its growth, challenges, and evolving opportunities.

International Cannabis Industry

The international cannabis industry has experienced significant growth and transformation in recent years, driven by changing regulations, shifting attitudes toward cannabis, and the recognition of its potential medical and economic benefits. Here's an overview of the global cannabis industry:

Legalization and Regulation: Many countries around the world have decriminalized or legalized cannabis for medical and/or recreational use. Some notable examples include Canada, Uruguay, and various European countries. Each jurisdiction has its own set of regulations governing cultivation, distribution, and consumption.

Medical Cannabis: The medical cannabis market has seen substantial expansion, with increasing acceptance of its therapeutic properties. Cannabis-derived medications, such as Epidiolex and Sativex, have gained approval for treating conditions like epilepsy and multiple sclerosis.

Recreational Use: Several countries and U.S. states have legalized cannabis for recreational purposes, leading to the emergence of a legal adult-use market. Notable examples include California, Colorado, and the Netherlands.

Investment and Market Growth: The cannabis industry has attracted significant investment, leading to the establishment of a robust supply chain. Cultivation, manufacturing, distribution, and retail sectors have all seen substantial growth.

Research and Development: Cannabis research has expanded, revealing potential medical applications beyond pain management and epilepsy, including mental health conditions, cancer treatment, and neurodegenerative diseases. This has opened new avenues for pharmaceutical and biotech companies.

Challenges: Despite growth, the global cannabis industry faces various challenges, including regulatory hurdles, taxation issues, banking limitations, and concerns about product quality and safety.

United States Cannabis Industry

Within the United States, the cannabis industry has undergone rapid development, with a patchwork of state-level regulations. Here's an overview of the U.S. cannabis industry:

Legalization by States: At last count, more than 40 U.S. states have legalized medical cannabis, and several have also legalized recreational use. These state-level regulations have created a complex landscape for businesses and consumers.

Economic Impact: The U.S. cannabis industry has become a significant economic driver, generating billions of dollars in revenue and thousands of jobs. Tax revenue from cannabis sales has funded various public programs in legal states.

Regulatory Variation: Regulations and licensing requirements vary widely from state to state. This inconsistency poses challenges for businesses aiming to operate in multiple states. Banking and Federal Law: Previously, federal law classified cannabis as a Schedule I controlled substance, making it challenging for cannabis businesses to access traditional banking services and exposing them to federal prosecution. With the DEA's reclassification of cannabis to a Schedule III drug as of April 2024, access to banking services may improve, although challenges will remain due to ongoing federal regulations. The reclassification is expected to reduce some financial risks associated with cannabis businesses, but the industry will need to navigate the evolving legal landscape carefully.

Social Equity: Many states have implemented social equity programs to address the historical injustices of the war on drugs. These programs aim to provide opportunities for individuals from marginalized communities to participate in the legal cannabis industry.

Product Diversity: The U.S. cannabis market offers a wide range of products, including flour, concentrates, edibles, topicals, and more. Product innovation and diversification have been key drivers of growth.

Ongoing Evolution: The U.S. cannabis industry continues to evolve as more states consider legalization and federal regulations change. With the DEA's recent decision to reclassify cannabis from a Schedule I to a Schedule III substance as of April 2024, the landscape is shifting. This rescheduling marks a significant federal acknowledgment of cannabis's medical benefits and lower abuse potential. The ongoing federal legalization efforts, including potential further changes in cannabis regulation, reflect a dynamic and rapidly changing industry that stakeholders must continually monitor and adapt to.

It's important to note that the cannabis industry is dynamic, and developments may have occurred during the publishing of this guide. Legal and market conditions can change rapidly, so individuals and businesses involved in the industry should stay informed about the latest developments and regulations in their specific regions.

LEGAL CONSIDERATIONS

DEA Rescheduling Impact: the DEA has rescheduled cannabis from Schedule I to Schedule III, a move reflecting a new federal stance on the drug's medicinal value and abuse potential. This reclassification affects numerous legal aspects, from reduced penalties for violations to expanded research opportunities, fundamentally altering compliance strategies for businesses.

The cannabis industry, both internationally and within the United States, operates within a complex web of legal considerations that shape every aspect of its operations. From licensing and regulatory compliance to the complications of federal prohibition, these legal factors have a profound impact on businesses operating in the sector. In this overview, we delve into the key legal considerations that cannabis operators face, offering insights into the legal requirements and challenges of participating in this ever-unfolding industry. From navigating international trade agreements to addressing state-by-state variations in the U.S., understanding these legal dynamics is essential for those seeking to thrive in the world of cannabis.

International Markets

Licensing and Regulatory Compliance: To participate as an operator in the international cannabis industry, businesses must obtain the necessary licenses and adhere to strict regulatory requirements. For instance, in Canada, companies must obtain licenses from Health Canada under the Cannabis Act and its regulations to cultivate, process, or sell cannabis.

Export and Import Regulations: Exporting and importing cannabis products across international borders require compliance with international trade agreements and the regulations of both the exporting and importing countries. Notable cases include Canada's export of medical cannabis to international markets.

Quality Control and Testing: Many countries mandate rigorous quality control and testing protocols to ensure the safety and potency of cannabis products. In Europe, the European Medicines Agency (EMA) sets standards for the quality of cannabis-derived medicinal products.

Intellectual Property and Patents: The cannabis industry sees increasing interest in intellectual property rights, including patents for unique cannabis strains, extraction methods, and delivery systems. Notable cases include GW Pharmaceuticals' patent for Epidiolex, a CBD-based medication.

International Trade Agreements: International trade agreements and treaties can impact the movement of cannabis products and related materials. Countries often navigate these agreements when establishing import and export regulations.

United States Market(s)

State Licensing: In states where cannabis is legalized, operators must obtain licenses for cultivation, manufacturing, distribution, and retail. For example, California's Bureau of Cannabis Control oversees licensing and compliance for various cannabis businesses.

Federal Prohibition and DEA's Rescheduling: Despite state-level legalization, cannabis remains regulated under federal law. Previously classified as a Schedule I controlled substance, cannabis was deemed to have a high potential for abuse and no accepted medical use. However, as of April 2024, the DEA has reclassified cannabis as a Schedule III drug, acknowledging its recognized medical benefits and lower abuse potential. This reclassification will significantly impact research opportunities, regulatory frameworks, and the overall cannabis market, facilitating a more favorable environment for the industry to grow and innovate.

Taxation: Cannabis businesses in the U.S. are subject to complex tax regulations, including Section 280E of the Internal Revenue Code, which disallows many deductions and credits for cannabis-related businesses, leading to higher tax burdens. The rescheduling to Schedule III will alter this provision, potentially allowing for more standard business deductions and reducing the effective tax rate for cannabis companies. Please continue to research and stay up to date on federal legalization consideration.

Social Equity Programs: Some states have implemented social equity programs to address historical injustices in cannabis enforcement. These programs often prioritize individuals from communities disproportionately impacted by the war on drugs.

Lab Testing and Product Labeling: States often require thorough lab testing for potency and contaminants, as well as detailed product labeling. Compliance with these requirements is crucial to avoid legal issues.

Banking and Financial Services: Cannabis businesses face challenges accessing traditional banking and financial services due to federal prohibition. The SAFE Banking Act is an example of proposed federal legislation aimed at addressing this issue. Rescheduling cannabis to Schedule III will improve access to banking services but will not fully eliminate associated risks.

Intellectual Property and Trademarks: Businesses in the U.S. cannabis industry face limitations on obtaining federal trademarks for cannabis-related products and services due to federal restrictions. Some have navigated this issue through creative branding and state-level trademarks.

Interstate Commerce: Interstate commerce of cannabis remains restricted, as cannabis products cannot legally cross state lines. The legal framework surrounding interstate commerce is a subject of ongoing debate and will be impacted by federal rescheduling.

Local Zoning and Land Use Regulations: Cannabis businesses must also comply with local zoning and land use regulations, which can vary significantly from one jurisdiction to another.

Legal considerations in the cannabis industry are complex and continually evolving. Businesses must stay informed about both federal and state-level regulations to successfully navigate this rapidly changing landscape. Notable cases and legal precedents can provide valuable insights into the evolving legal landscape. Stay ahead of the curve and up to date.

QUICK START GUIDE

Welcome to the world of cannabis entrepreneurship! This quick-start guide is designed to help you, a novice in the cannabis industry, navigate the initial stages of starting your business. Follow these critical steps to lay a solid foundation for your venture.

Understand the Cannabis Industry

Research: Start with understanding the basics of cannabis, including different strains, products, and their uses. Familiarize yourself with the current market trends, consumer demands, and future growth prospects.

Legal Landscape: Gain a clear understanding of the legalities surrounding cannabis in your area. Laws vary significantly by state and country, affecting how you can operate your business.

Create a Business Plan: Draft a business plan that outlines your vision, mission, target market, competitive analysis, financial projections, and operational plans. A well-thought-out business plan is crucial for clarity and securing funding.

Secure Licenses and Permits: Research and apply for the necessary licenses and permits required to operate a cannabis business in your jurisdiction. This step can be time-consuming and complex, so start early.

Funding Your Business: Explore various funding options, including private investors, loans, and crowdfunding. Prepare a pitch that highlights the unique aspects of your business to attract potential investors.

Choose Your Location Wisely: Select a location for your business that complies with local zoning laws and is accessible to your target market. Consider the costs and logistics involved in setting up your operation.

Establish Relationships with Suppliers: For retail operations, build relationships with reputable suppliers to ensure a consistent and high-quality product supply. For cultivation, invest in quality seeds, nutrients, and equipment.

Market Your Business: Develop a marketing plan that complies with regulations yet effectively reaches your target audience. Consider digital marketing, educational content, and community engagement as part of your strategy.

Launch and Learn: Prepare for a soft launch to evaluate your operations, gather feedback, and make necessary adjustments. Always be open to learning and evolving your business based on market demands and regulatory changes.

BUSINESS START-UP GUIDELINES

Welcome to the foundational guide of starting your own cannabis business. As you embark on this exciting venture, it's essential to approach each step with diligence and a keen eye for detail. This guide is tailored to help novice entrepreneurs navigate the complexities of the cannabis industry, providing you with a clear roadmap to laying the groundwork for a successful business.

First Steps for Novices: Embarking on a cannabis business requires careful planning and an understanding of the unique landscape of the industry. Start with these crucial steps:

Understanding Your Local Cannabis Market: Research is key. Identify your target market; understand their needs, preferences, and the competitive landscape.

Navigating Legal Requirements: Familiarize yourself with the legal framework surrounding cannabis businesses in your jurisdiction. This includes understanding licensing, zoning, and compliance requirements.

Crafting an Initial Business Plan: Develop a concise business plan that outlines your business objectives, strategies for market entry, and financial projections. This document will be your roadmap and can help secure funding.

Estimating Your Startup Costs

A critical component of your planning process involves understanding and estimating the startup costs associated with launching a cannabis business.

These costs can vary significantly based on the type of operation you intend to start (cultivation, retail dispensary, etc.).

Cultivation Startup Costs: Initial investment can range significantly based on scale and location. Small operations may require $50,000 to $100,000, while larger facilities might need upwards of $1 million, covering equipment, licensing fees, and facility costs.

Dispensary Startup Costs: Opening a dispensary typically involves substantial investment, from $150,000 to $2 million, encompassing leasing, inventory, staffing, and security.

Budgeting Tips: Creating a detailed and realistic budget is paramount. Your budget should account for all initial expenses, operational costs, and an additional buffer for unforeseen expenses. Utilize budgeting software or templates designed for small businesses to maintain financial oversight.

Financial Resources

Engage with the Community: Join online forums and platforms where experienced cannabis entrepreneurs share insights, advice, and support. These communities can be invaluable resources for navigating early-stage challenges.

Expert Financial Advice: Seeking advice from financial advisors experienced in the cannabis sector is highly recommended. Prepare to discuss:

- ✓ Common financial hurdles for cannabis startups and strategies to overcome them.

- ✓ Effective ways to present your business to potential investors and lenders.

Funding Your Venture

Understanding your funding options is crucial for getting your business off the ground. Explore different avenues:

Private Investors: While they may offer significant capital, they'll likely want a stake in your business.

Loans: Though traditional bank loans may be challenging, specialized private lenders offer alternatives.

Crowdfunding: This method allows you to raise funds from a broad audience, mitigating the need for large individual investors.

Cannabis-Specific Grants: Investigate state or privately funded grants available for cannabis startups, particularly those with a focus on medical use.

Note: By following these guidelines and leveraging the suggested resources from this guide, you're well on your way to turning your cannabis business vision into reality. Remember, the key to success lies in thorough preparation, strategic planning, and continuous learning.

STEP-BY-STEP GUIDE: STARTING AND RUNNING A CULTIVATION FACILITY AND WHOLESALE BUSINESS

This section provides a comprehensive guide on establishing and managing a cannabis cultivation and wholesale business, covering legal and regulatory compliance, facility location and design, cultivation methods, quality control, distribution strategies, and technology integration. It emphasizes the importance of understanding market demands, maintaining product quality, and ensuring operational efficiency to succeed in the competitive cannabis industry.

Step 1: Assess Legal and Regulatory Requirements

- ✓ Research and understand local, state, and federal regulations governing cannabis cultivation and wholesale distribution.

- ✓ Identify licensing requirements and application procedures for both cultivation and wholesale activities.

Step 2: Choose an Ideal Location for Cultivation Facility

- ✓ Select a location that complies with zoning regulations and provides optimal climate conditions for cultivation.

- ✓ Consider factors such as proximity to markets and ease of transportation for wholesale distribution.

Step 3: Licensing and Compliance

- ✓ Navigate the licensing process for cultivation and wholesale activities.

- ✓ Develop and implement stringent compliance protocols to adhere to all regulations.

Step 4: Facility Design and Setup for Cultivation

- ✓ Design an efficient and secure cultivation facility, considering layout, lighting, ventilation, and security.

- ✓ Invest in advanced cultivation technology, including climate control systems and irrigation.

Step 5: Cultivation Process

- ✓ Choose the right cannabis strains based on market demand and cultivation capabilities.

- ✓ Implement sustainable and efficient cultivation practices, including soil or hydroponic methods.

- ✓ Develop pest and disease management strategies.

- ✓ Establish protocols for harvesting, drying, and curing.

Step 6: Product Quality Control and Testing

- ✓ Implement rigorous quality control measures for cultivation.

- ✓ Establish partnerships with testing laboratories to ensure product compliance and safety.

Step 7: Inventory Management for Cultivation

- ✓ Implement robust inventory tracking systems to monitor strain availability, growth cycles, and harvesting schedules.

Step 8: Facility Design and Setup for Wholesale Distribution

- ✓ Design a distribution facility with efficient storage, packaging, and shipping capabilities.

- ✓ Implement security measures for wholesale distribution, including surveillance systems.

Step 9: Wholesale Distribution Strategy

- ✓ Develop a wholesale pricing strategy that is competitive and aligns with market demands.

- ✓ Establish relationships with dispensaries, retailers, and other wholesale buyers.

- ✓ Explore online platforms for wholesale distribution.

Step 10: Compliance in Wholesale Distribution

- ✓ Ensure all wholesale transactions comply with local and state regulations.

- ✓ Implement measures for accurate record-keeping and compliance checks.

Step 11: Technology Integration

- ✓ Utilize technology for inventory management, order processing, and distribution tracking.

- ✓ Consider implementing an online portal for wholesale orders and communication.

Step 12: Branding and Marketing for Wholesale Business

- ✓ Develop a strong brand identity for your wholesale business.

- ✓ Implement marketing strategies to promote your wholesale offerings, including industry events and digital marketing.

Step 13: Continuous Improvement

- ✓ Encourage a culture of continuous improvement within cultivation and distribution operations.

✓ Regularly assess and optimize cultivation processes and wholesale distribution strategies.

Step 14: Network within the Industry

✓ Attend industry events, conferences, and networking opportunities.

✓ Build relationships with other cultivators, wholesalers, and industry stakeholders.

Step 15: Sustainability Initiatives

✓ Consider implementing sustainable practices in cultivation and wholesale operations.

Step 16: Stay Informed and Adapt

✓ Stay abreast of industry trends, regulatory changes, and emerging products.

✓ Adapt your business strategies to remain competitive and compliant.

Step 17: Evaluate and Expand

✓ Regularly assess the performance of your cultivation and wholesale business against key metrics.

✓ Explore opportunities for expansion or diversification based on market trends.

Step 18: Community Engagement

✓ Engage with the local community through events, sponsorships, and partnerships.

CHECKLIST FOR OBTAINING A CULTIVATION LICENSE

This section outlines a detailed process for obtaining a cannabis cultivation license, covering regulatory familiarization, eligibility verification, license type selection, business plan development, location securing, security and compliance planning, financial preparation, application submission, review, inspection, public commenting, regulatory decision, and post-licensing compliance. It provides a framework for applicants to navigate the complexities of licensing, emphasizing the importance of thorough preparation and adherence to regulations.

Step 1: Familiarize Yourself with Regulations

Objective: Understand federal, state, and local regulations governing cannabis cultivation.

Actions:

❑ Review relevant laws and regulations.

❑ Attend informational sessions or workshops hosted by the regulatory authority.

Step 2: Identify Eligibility Criteria

Objective: Ensure that the applicant meets eligibility requirements.

Actions:

❑ Verify minimum age, residency, and criminal background check criteria.

❑ Confirm financial stability and capacity to operate a cultivation facility.

Step 3: Choose the Type of Cultivation License

Objective: Determine the specific type of cultivation license required.

Actions:

- ❑ Understand and choose between indoor, outdoor, or greenhouse cultivation.

- ❑ Select the cultivation tier (e.g., small, medium, large) based on production capacity.

Step 4: Develop a Comprehensive Business Plan

Objective: Provide a detailed plan outlining your cultivation operations.

Actions:

- ❑ Include information on facility design, security measures, and cultivation methods.

- ❑ Outline staffing, quality control, and community engagement strategies.

Step 5: Secure a Suitable Location

Objective: Identify and secure a location compliant with zoning regulations.

Actions:

- ❑ Confirm the property's eligibility for cannabis cultivation.

- ❑ Address any local zoning restrictions.

Step 6: Build a Security and Compliance Plan

Objective: Develop robust plans for security and regulatory compliance.

Actions:

- ❑ Detailed security measures to prevent unauthorized access and theft.

- ❑ Outline procedures to ensure compliance with cultivation regulations.

Step 7: Financial Planning and Documentation

Objective: Demonstrate fiscal responsibility and stability.

Actions:

- ❑ Prepare financial statements and budgets.

- ❑ Provide evidence of funding sources and financial viability.

Step 8: Application Submission

Objective: Submit a comprehensive application to the regulatory authority.

Actions:

- ❑ Complete the application form with accurate and detailed information.

- ❑ Include all required documents and fees.

Step 9: Application Review and Verification

Objective: The regulatory authority reviews and verifies the submitted application.

Actions:

- ❑ Conduct thorough background checks on applicants.

- ❑ Verify the accuracy of the information provided.

Step 10: Inspection and Site Visit

Objective: Assess the suitability of the proposed cultivation facility.

Actions:

- ❑ Conduct on-site inspections to ensure compliance with regulations.

- ❑ Evaluate security measures, facility layout, and cultivation practices.

Step 11: Public Comment Period (if applicable)

Objective: Allow community input on the proposed cultivation operation.

Actions:

- ❑ Notify the public and stakeholders of the proposed cultivation license.

- ❑ Provide a designated period for public comments or concerns.

Step 12: Regulatory Decision

Objective: The regulatory authority decides on the cultivation license.

Actions:

- ❑ Approve or deny the application based on compliance, suitability, and public input.

- ❑ Communicate the decision to you, the applicant.

Step 13: Licensing and Compliance Period

Objective: If approved, initiate the licensing process, and ensure ongoing compliance.

Actions:

- ❑ Obtain your cultivation license.

- ❑ Monitor your ongoing operations for adherence to regulations.

STEP-BY-STEP GUIDE: STARTING AND RUNNING A MEDICAL AND RECREATIONAL DISPENSARY

This section provides a detailed guide for launching and managing both medical and recreational cannabis dispensaries. It covers the entire process from understanding legal requirements, selecting a suitable location, ensuring compliance, designing the facility, managing inventory, staffing, educating customers, branding, integrating technology, engaging with the community, and continuously improving operations and compliance to adapt to the evolving cannabis industry landscape.

Step 1: Assess Legal and Regulatory Landscape:

- ✓ Research and understand the local, state, and federal regulations governing medical and recreational cannabis dispensaries.

- ✓ Identify licensing requirements and application procedures.

Step 2: Choose an Ideal Location

- ✓ Select a location that complies with zoning regulations and is accessible to your target market.

- ✓ Consider factors such as visibility, foot traffic, and proximity to competitors.

Step 3: Licensing and Compliance

- ✓ Navigate the licensing process, ensuring compliance with all regulations.

- ✓ Develop and implement stringent compliance protocols for both medical and recreational sales.

Step 4: Facility Design and Setup

- ✓ Design an inviting and secure retail space, considering layout and interior design.

- ✓ Invest in high-quality security systems to comply with regulatory requirements.

Step 5: Product Sourcing and Inventory Management

- ✓ Establish relationships with reputable cannabis suppliers.

- ✓ Implement robust inventory management systems to track product quantities and expiration dates.

Step 6: Staffing and Training

- ✓ Hire knowledgeable and customer-focused staff with expertise in cannabis products.

- ✓ Provide comprehensive training on product knowledge, customer service, and compliance.

Step 7: Customer Education

- ✓ Develop educational materials to inform customers about different cannabis products, consumption methods, and dosages.

- ✓ Train staff to offer personalized recommendations based on customer needs.

Step 8: Marketing and Branding

- ✓ Create a distinctive brand identity that aligns with your values and resonates with your target audience.

- ✓ Implement a strategic marketing plan, leveraging online and offline channels.

Step 9: Security and Compliance

- ✓ Implement stringent security measures to safeguard your dispensary and inventory.

- ✓ Regularly audit and update compliance protocols to adapt to changing regulations.

Step 10: Technology Integration

- ✓ Utilize POS systems and inventory management software for streamlined operations.

- ✓ Consider online ordering and delivery options for enhanced customer convenience.

Step 11: Community Engagement

- ✓ Engage with the local community through events, sponsorships, and partnerships.

- ✓ Establish a positive public image through social responsibility initiatives.

Step 12: Ongoing Compliance and Quality Control

- ✓ Regularly update staff training programs to ensure ongoing compliance.

- ✓ Implement quality control measures to maintain product consistency and safety.

Step 13: Customer Relationship Management (CRM)

- ✓ Utilize CRM systems to track customer preferences, purchase history, and feedback.

- ✓ Implement loyalty programs to reward repeat customers.

Step 14: Stay Informed and Adapt

- ✓ Stay abreast of industry trends, regulatory changes, and emerging products.

- ✓ Adapt your business strategies to remain competitive and compliant.

Step 15: Continuous Improvement

- ✓ Encourage a culture of continuous improvement among your staff.

- ✓ Seek customer feedback and use it to enhance your products and services.

Step 16: Network within the Industry

- ✓ Attend industry events, conferences, and networking opportunities.

- ✓ Collaborate with other industry professionals to stay connected and informed.

Step 17: Sustainability Initiatives

- ✓ Consider implementing sustainable practices, such as recycling programs and eco-friendly packaging.

Step 18: Evaluate and Expand

- ✓ Regularly assess your dispensary's performance against key metrics.

- ✓ Explore opportunities for expansion or diversification based on market trends.

CHECKLIST FOR OBTAINING A RETAIL AND MEDICAL LICENSE

This section outlines a systematic approach for obtaining cannabis retail and medical licenses, covering regulatory understanding, eligibility confirmation, license type selection, business plan development, location securing, security and compliance planning, financial preparation, application submission and review, inspections, public commenting, regulatory decision-making, and maintaining compliance. It serves as a comprehensive guide for applicants to navigate the licensing process in the cannabis industry.

Step 1: Understand Regulatory Landscape

Objective: Gain a comprehensive understanding of federal, state, and local regulations governing cannabis retail and medical operations.

Actions:

- ❑ Review and comprehend relevant cannabis laws and regulations.

- ❑ Attend regulatory workshops or informational sessions.

Step 2: Confirm Eligibility

Objective: Ensure the applicant meets eligibility criteria for both retail and medical licensing.

Actions:

- ❑ Verify minimum age, residency, and criminal background check requirements.

❑ Confirm financial stability and ability to operate a retail and medical cannabis facility.

Step 3: Choose License Type

Objective: Determine the specific type of retail and medical licenses required.

Actions:

❑ Differentiate between adult-use (recreational) and medical cannabis licenses.

❑ Choose the appropriate license categories, such as dispensary, delivery, or both.

Step 4: Develop a Comprehensive Business Plan

Objective: Present a detailed plan outlining the retail and medical cannabis operations.

Actions:

❑ Include information on store design, security measures, and product offerings.

❑ Outline staffing, patient education, and community engagement strategies for medical operations.

Step 5: Secure Suitable Location

Objective: Identify and secure a location compliant with zoning regulations for both retail and medical cannabis.

Actions:

❑ Confirm the property's eligibility for cannabis retail and medical operations.

❑   Address any local zoning restrictions.

Step 6: Build a Security and Compliance Plan

Objective: Develop robust plans for security and regulatory compliance in both retail and medical operations.

Actions:

❑   Detailed security measures to prevent unauthorized access and theft.

❑   Outline procedures to ensure compliance with retail and medical cannabis regulations.

Step 7: Financial Planning and Documentation

Objective: Demonstrate financial responsibility and stability for both retail and medical cannabis operations.

Actions:

❑   Prepare financial statements and budgets.

❑   Provide evidence of funding sources and financial viability.

Step 8: Application Submission

Objective: Submit a comprehensive application for both retail and medical licenses to the regulatory authority.

Actions:

❑   Complete the application forms with accurate and detailed information.

❑   Include all required documents, fees, and supporting materials.

Step 9: Application Review and Verification

Objective: The regulatory authority reviews and verifies the submitted application for both retail and medical licenses.

Actions:

❑ Conduct thorough background checks on applicants.

❑ Verify the accuracy of the information provided.

Step 10: Inspection and Site Visit

Objective: Assess the suitability of the proposed retail and medical cannabis facilities.

Actions:

❑ Conduct on-site inspections to ensure compliance with regulations.

❑ Evaluate security measures, facility layout, and adherence to medical cannabis guidelines.

Step 11: Public Comment Period (if applicable)

Objective: Allow community input on the proposed retail and medical cannabis operations.

Actions:

❑ Notify the public and stakeholders of the proposed retail and medical license.

❑ Provide a designated period for public comments or concerns.

Step 12: Regulatory Decision

Objective: The regulatory authority decides on both retail and medical cannabis licenses.

Actions:

❑ Approve or deny the application based on compliance, suitability, and public input.

❑ Communicate the decision to you, the applicant.

Step 13: Licensing and Compliance Period

Objective: If approved, initiate the licensing process for both retail and medical cannabis and ensure ongoing compliance.

Actions:

❑ Obtain your retail and/or medical cannabis licenses.

❑ Monitor your ongoing operations for adherence to regulations.

MARKETING FOR DISPENSARY OR CULTIVATION BUSINESS

Effective marketing is crucial for the success of any business, including those in the cannabis industry. Due to the unique regulatory landscape, cannabis businesses must navigate a variety of restrictions and guidelines when developing their marketing strategies. Below, we've expanded on compliant marketing strategies with practical examples to help your cannabis dispensary or cultivation business thrive while adhering to regulations.

Understanding Your Target Audience

Demographic Analysis: Conduct in-depth research to understand the age, preferences, and consumption habits of your target market.

Customer Personas: Create detailed customer personas to tailor your marketing strategies effectively.

Building a Strong Brand Identity

Consistent Messaging: Ensure your brand's message is clear, consistent, and reflects your company's values and mission.

Logo and Design: Design a memorable logo and visual theme that can be used across all marketing materials and channels.

Digital Marketing Strategies

Educational Content: Create and share valuable content that educates your audience about cannabis products, their benefits, and safe consumption practices. This can include blog posts, infographics, and informative videos.

SEO Practices: Optimize your website and content for search engines to increase visibility. Focus on cannabis-related keywords that are frequently searched by your target audience.

Social Media Marketing: Utilize platforms where cannabis marketing is permitted, focusing on educational and lifestyle content rather than direct promotion of cannabis products. Engage with your followers through regular posts, stories, and interactive sessions.

Email Marketing

Newsletter Signups: Encourage website visitors to sign up for your newsletter for updates, offers, and educational content. Ensure compliance by including age verification.

Segmentation: Segment your email list to send targeted campaigns that cater to different customer preferences and behaviors.

Community Engagement and Events

Sponsor Local Events: Engage with your community by sponsoring or participating in local events that align with your brand values. This can include wellness fairs, music festivals, and educational seminars.

Host Workshops: Offer workshops or seminars on topics related to cannabis, such as cooking with cannabis, understanding different strains, or the science behind cannabis. Ensure these events comply with local regulations regarding cannabis promotion and consumption.

Loyalty Programs

Rewards for Repeat Customers: Implement a loyalty program that rewards repeat customers with discounts, exclusive offers, or early access to new products. This encourages ongoing engagement and brand loyalty.

Partnerships and Collaborations

Collaborate with Influencers: Partner with influencers who align with your brand's values and can legally promote cannabis-related content. Ensure any influencer partnerships comply with platform guidelines and local regulations.

Cross-Promotions with Non-Cannabis Businesses: Partner with local businesses that offer complementary products or services, such as wellness centers, cafes, or yoga studios, for cross-promotional efforts.

NOTE: By incorporating these compliant marketing strategies, your cannabis business can effectively reach and engage your target audience, build brand loyalty, and drive growth while navigating the complexities of cannabis marketing regulations. Always stay updated on the latest guidelines and seek legal advice to ensure all your marketing efforts are fully compliant.

TAX AND ACCOUNTING

Navigating the tax and accounting landscape of the cannabis industry can be daunting, especially with complex regulations like Section 280E of the Internal Revenue Service (IRS) code. Here's a simplified breakdown to help you understand the basics and a step-by-step guide for preparing your financial projections.

What is Section 280E?

Imagine you have a lemonade stand, but there's a rule that says you can't deduct the cost of sugar, cups, or lemons from your earnings when calculating your taxes. That's similar to what Section 280E does to cannabis businesses. It says that if your business involves federally illegal substances (like cannabis), you can't deduct most of your business expenses when you do your taxes. This rule can make your taxable income look higher than it really is, leading to higher taxes.

Why does it matter?

For cannabis businesses, this means paying taxes on gross profits rather than net profits, significantly increasing tax obligations.

While Section 280E limits deductions, you're still allowed to subtract the cost of goods sold. This includes the direct costs associated with producing your cannabis products (like seeds, soil, and direct labor).

STEP-BY-STEP GUIDE: 280E
FINANCIAL PROJECTIONS

Step 1: Estimate Your Sales

- ✓ Start by estimating how much cannabis you expect to sell. Consider factors like your business size, location, and customer base.

Step 2: Calculate Cost of Goods Sold (COGS)

- ✓ List all the direct costs involved in producing your cannabis products. This can include purchasing seeds, growing materials, and direct labor costs. Add these up to get your total COGS.

Step 3: Determine Gross Profit

- ✓ Subtract your COGS from your estimated sales to find your gross profit. This is your revenue before operating expenses, taxes, and interest.

Step 4: Identify Operating Expenses

- ✓ Though you can't deduct most operating expenses due to Section 280E, it's still important to know them for managing your business.

- ✓ List expenses like rent, utilities, marketing, and salaries (other than those included in COGS).

Step 5: Calculate Your Taxable Income:

- ✓ Subtract COGS from your gross profit to determine your taxable income under Section 280E. Remember, operating expenses aren't subtracted here due to the IRS rule.

Step 6: Estimate Your Taxes

✓ Apply the appropriate tax rate to your taxable income to estimate your tax liability. Keep in mind, this rate will depend on your business structure (e.g., LLC, corporation).

Step 7: Adjust for Non-Deductible Expenses

✓ Finally, adjust your financial planning to account for the inability to deduct many operating expenses. This adjustment helps you understand your true financial position and plan for cash flow needs.

Tips for Managing Finances Under Section 280E

Keep Detailed Records: Meticulous record-keeping is crucial for substantiating your COGS and staying compliant.

Seek Professional Advice: Consulting with a tax professional experienced in the cannabis industry can help navigate these complex tax laws effectively.

Explore Legal Structures: Different business structures can impact your tax obligations. Discuss with an advisor to find the best setup for your situation.

Understanding and planning around Section 280E can be challenging. With careful management and strategic planning, your cannabis business can navigate these tax waters successfully. Always stay informed about potential tax law changes and consider professional advice for your specific situation.

SUCCESS STORIES

Emma's Edibles Journey: Emma started her cannabis edibles company with a passion for cooking and a belief in cannabis as a beneficial supplement. Facing initial challenges with funding and navigating regulations, she focused on creating unique, high-quality products. By attending industry events and leveraging social media marketing within legal guidelines, Emma's Edibles gained popularity. Today, her products are stocked in dispensaries across three states, a testament to the power of perseverance and innovation in the cannabis industry.

Green Thumb Cultivation: Mark and Lisa, a couple with a background in horticulture, ventured into cannabis cultivation. They began their journey with a small, carefully selected crop and focused on sustainable growing practices. Despite early challenges, including crop diseases and market fluctuations, their commitment to quality and sustainability set them apart. Green Thumb Cultivation now supplies premium organic cannabis to several dispensaries, and they've expanded their operation to include educational tours about sustainable cultivation practices.

Canoja Technologies: We started Canoja with a vision of being at the forefront of cannabis technology innovation, providing cutting-edge tools and solutions to streamline operations, enhance compliance, and drive business success within the cannabis industry. By leveraging advanced software platforms and industry expertise, Canoja empowers businesses to thrive in a competitive and regulated market.

Learn more about Canoja Technologies and their offerings by visiting their website: www.canoja.com.

RESOURCES, REFERENCES AND TEMPLATES

The reference section is a compendium of valuable resources for individuals and businesses operating in the cannabis industry. It provides a detailed list of various cannabis-related organizations, websites, and services ranging from technology solutions, industry associations, and legal services to marketing and accounting firms. These resources are instrumental for anyone looking to navigate the complex landscape of the cannabis industry, offering insights into legal compliance, business strategies, industry trends, and networking opportunities. Additionally, it highlights the significance of staying current with evolving regulations and market dynamics, emphasizing the need for continuous learning and adaptation in this rapidly growing field.

CHECKLIST FOR STARTING A CANNABIS BUSINESS

This section offers a detailed checklist for starting a cannabis business, covering research, business plan development, legal compliance, securing funding, facility setup, cultivation and production, team building, retail operations, marketing, networking, and staying informed. It emphasizes the importance of understanding regulations, developing a strong business strategy, ensuring legal and financial readiness, focusing on quality, and engaging with the cannabis community.

Research and Education:

❑ Understand local cannabis regulations.

❑ Stay informed about industry trends and market dynamics.

Business Plan Development:

❑ Define the type of cannabis business (cultivation, processing, dispensary, etc.).

❑ Conduct market analysis to identify the target audience, competition, and trends.

❑ Develop a detailed financial plan, including startup costs and revenue projections.

Legal Compliance:

❑ Consult with attorneys experienced in cannabis law.

❑ Understand and initiate the licensing process.

- ❑ Submit all required documents for licensing.

Secure Funding:

- ❑ Assess financial needs for licensing, facility setup, and initial operations.

- ❑ Explore funding options such as investors, loans, or partnerships.

Facility Setup:

- ❑ Choose a location compliant with zoning regulations.

- ❑ Implement adequate security measures.

- ❑ Invest in necessary equipment and technology.

Cultivation and Production:

- ❑ Secure the required cultivation license.

- ❑ Develop and implement standard operating procedures (SOPs) for cultivation and processing.

- ❑ Focus on quality control and sustainable practices.

Build a Professional Team:

- ❑ Assemble a skilled team with expertise in cultivation, processing, compliance, and sales.

- ❑ Provide ongoing training for the team.

Retail Operations:

- ❑ Obtain the necessary dispensary license.

- ❑ Train staff to educate customers about cannabis products and compliance.

- ❑ Create a welcoming and compliant retail environment.

Marketing and Branding:

- ❑ Establish a unique and compliant brand identity.

- ❑ Utilize online platforms for marketing, adhering to advertising regulations.

- ❑ Engage in community events and sponsorships.

Networking and Industry Involvement:

- ❑ Join cannabis industry associations for networking.

- ❑ Attend relevant conferences, trade shows, and events.

Adapt and Stay Informed:

- ❑ Stay flexible and adapt your business model to changing regulations and market dynamics.

- ❑ Continuously learn about industry updates, new technologies, and emerging trends.

NOTE: This checklist provides a comprehensive guide for the key steps involved in starting a cannabis business. Adjust and customize it based on the specific requirements of your location and business model. Remember to regularly review and update your business plan as needed.

CANNABIS RESOURCES AND ORGANIZATIONS

This section provides a compilation of essential resources and organizations relevant to the cannabis industry, offering guidance, support, and networking opportunities for businesses and individuals. It may include regulatory bodies, industry associations, educational platforms, and advocacy groups that play a pivotal role in the development, compliance, and advancement of cannabis enterprises.

Canoja

Website: http://Canoja.com/

National Cannabis Industry Association (NCIA)

Website: https://thecannabisindustry.org/

Marijuana Business Daily (MJBizDaily)

Website: https://mjbizdaily.com/

Leafly

Website: https://www.leafly.com/

Cannabis Business Executive (CBE)

Website: https://www.cannabisbusinessexecutive.com/

American Cannabis Nurses Association (ACNA)

Website: https://www.cannabisnurses.org/

Hemp Industries Association (HIA)

Website: https://thehia.org/

Open Cannabis Project

Website: https://opencannabisproject.org/

Cannabis Marketing Association (CMA)

Website: https://thecannabismarketingassociation.com/

Society of Cannabis Clinicians (SCC)

Website: https://www.cannabisclinicians.org/

Cannabis Science Conference

Website: https://www.cannabisscienceconference.com/

National Organization for the Reform of Marijuana Laws (NORML)

Website: https://norml.org/

Cannabis Cultivation and Science Podcast

Website: https://www.cannabissciencetoday.com/

International Cannabis Farmers Association (ICFA)

Website: https://internationalcannabisfarmers.org/

Cannabis Alliance (CA)

Website: https://www.cannabisalliance.org/

Cannabis Training University

Website: https://cannabistraininguniversity.com/

Minorities for Medical Marijuana (M4MM)

Website: https://minorities4medicalmarijuana.org/

Cannabis Control Commission (CCC) - Massachusetts

Website: https://masscannabiscontrol.com/

Cannabis Council of Canada

Website: https://cannabis-council.ca/

European Industrial Hemp Association (EIHA)

Website: https://eiha.org/

National Hemp Association

Website: https://nationalhempassociation.org/

HyMind Media Podcast and Guides

Website: https://hymindmedia.com

NOTE: This list includes a variety of resources, from industry associations to educational platforms, which can help you stay informed, connect with professionals, and navigate the dynamic landscape of the cannabis industry. Be sure to explore these resources to enhance your knowledge and network within the cannabis community.

ATTORNEYS AND LEGAL REPRESENTATION

This section provides information on finding and engaging attorneys and legal representation specialized in the cannabis industry. It may offer insights on selecting legal professionals experienced in navigating the complex regulatory landscape of cannabis businesses, including compliance, licensing, and business structuring, ensuring that enterprises operate within the legal frameworks at federal, state, and local levels.

Legal Directories: Explore legal directories such as Avvo, Martindale-Hubbell, or FindLaw. These directories allow you to search for attorneys by location and practice area.

State Bar Associations: Visit the official website of the state bar association in the specific state in which you are interested. Most state bar associations have directories of attorneys practicing in different areas.

Networking: Attend industry events, conferences, or local meetups related to cannabis. Networking with professionals in the industry can lead to recommendations for legal services.

Referrals: Ask for referrals from other business owners or professionals in the cannabis industry. Personal recommendations can be valuable in finding an attorney with relevant experience.

Legal Cannabis Organizations: Reach out to legal organizations specifically focused on cannabis law. They may have resources or directories of attorneys specializing in cannabis-related legal matters.

Online Forums and Communities: Participate in online forums or communities related to cannabis business. Members of these communities may share recommendations for attorneys.

Consultations: Consider scheduling consultations with potential attorneys to discuss your specific needs, get a sense of their expertise, and determine if they are the right fit for your business.

NOTE: Remember to verify the credentials and experience of any attorney you consider hiring. Cannabis law is a specialized field, so finding an attorney with experience in this area is crucial. Additionally, laws and regulations regarding cannabis can vary widely, so it is important to work with someone familiar with the specific regulations in the state where your business operates.

TIPS FOR FINDING CANNABIS MARKETING AND ACCOUNTING FIRMS

This section offers guidance on how to identify and select specialized marketing and accounting firms within the cannabis industry. It could provide tips on evaluating firms' expertise in navigating the unique challenges and opportunities in cannabis marketing and financial management, ensuring compliance with industry-specific regulations, and leveraging market trends for business growth.

Industry Directories: Explore industry-specific directories and databases that list cannabis-related service providers. Examples include Leafly's cannabis directory, Weedmaps, and industry association websites.

Online Search: Use search engines to find marketing and accounting firms that specialize in the cannabis industry. Include specific keywords such as "cannabis marketing agency" or "cannabis accounting services" along with your location.

Industry Events and Conferences: Attend cannabis industry events and conferences where you can meet and connect with marketing and accounting professionals who specialize in the cannabis sector.

Networking: Connect with professionals in the cannabis industry through networking platforms like LinkedIn. Ask for recommendations from colleagues or industry contacts.

Trade Associations: Explore cannabis trade associations and organizations. They often have lists of recommended service providers or may provide referrals upon request.

LIST OF CANNABIS MARKETING AND ACCOUNTING FIRMS

This section provides a curated list of reputable cannabis marketing and accounting firms, showcasing their expertise in supporting businesses within the cannabis industry. It highlights firms known for their specialized services in branding, digital marketing, financial management, and regulatory compliance, offering links to their websites for further information. This resource is valuable for cannabis businesses seeking professional assistance in navigating the complex landscape of marketing and financial regulations specific to the cannabis sector.

Cannabis Marketing Firms:

Wick & Mortar: https://wickandmortar.com/

CannaVerse Solutions: https://www.cannaversesolutions.com/

Cannabrand: https://cannabrand.co/

Cannabis Accounting Firms:

Bridge West CPAs: https://bridgewestcpas.com/

GreenGrowth CPAs: https://greengrowthcpas.com/

NOTE: The status and prominence of these firms may have changed since my last update, and new firms may have emerged. Always conduct your own research, check reviews, and consider consulting with firms directly to ensure they align with your specific needs and goals. Additionally, the legal landscape for cannabis is subject to change, so be sure to collaborate with professionals well-versed in current regulations.

COMMON REQUIREMENTS FOR OBTAINING A CANNABIS LICENSE

This section outlines the common requirements for obtaining a cannabis license, emphasizing the need for a thorough understanding of local and state regulations. It covers legal age, residency, background checks, financial stability, comprehensive business planning, security measures, zoning compliance, property information, standard operating procedures, quality control, environmental standards, community engagement, regulatory compliance, insurance, employee training, and tax obligations. It underscores the dynamic nature of cannabis laws and the importance of continuous learning and professional guidance in the licensing process.

The requirements for obtaining a cannabis license vary significantly depending on the jurisdiction, as cannabis laws are determined at the state or even local level. It is crucial to thoroughly research and understand the specific regulations in the jurisdiction where you intend to operate. However, I can provide a general overview of common requirements often associated with obtaining a cannabis license.

Legal Age and Residency: Applicants must typically be of legal age (18 or 21, depending on the jurisdiction) and may be required to be residents of the state or region.

Background Checks: Applicants and key personnel may undergo thorough background checks, including criminal history, financial background, and any relevant industry experience.

Financial Requirements: Applicants may need to demonstrate financial stability and have the necessary capital to establish and operate a cannabis business. Financial disclosure documents may be required.

Business Plan: A comprehensive business plan outlining the details of the proposed cannabis business, including its structure, operations, marketing strategy, and financial projections.

Security Measures: Plans for security measures to safeguard the premises, product, and personnel. This may include surveillance systems, access controls, and alarm systems.

Zoning Compliance: Verification that the proposed location for the cannabis business complies with local zoning regulations. This may involve obtaining approval from local authorities.

Land Use and Property Information: Details about the property, including ownership information, lease agreements, and proof of property compliance with state and local regulations.

Standard Operating Procedures (SOPs): Comprehensive SOPs detailing the day-to-day operations of the cannabis business, including cultivation, processing, and dispensing procedures.

Quality Control and Testing Plans: Plans to ensure the quality and safety of cannabis products, including testing procedures and compliance with quality standards.

Environmental Compliance: Demonstrating adherence to environmental regulations, waste disposal plans, and sustainable business practices.

Community Engagement and Support: Some jurisdictions may require evidence of community support for the cannabis business, which may involve public hearings or outreach programs.

Compliance with State Regulations: Strict adherence to state-specific cannabis regulations, which may cover licensing fees, product labeling, advertising restrictions, and more.

Insurance: Obtaining the required insurance coverage, such as liability insurance, to operate a cannabis business.

Employee Training: Plans for training employees on cannabis regulations, safety protocols, and responsible business practices.

Tax Compliance: Demonstrating an understanding of and compliance with tax regulations, including sales tax and excise tax obligations.

NOTE: Most cannabis licenses are awarded based on a scoring system. Therefore, it is crucial to score high on each section to increase the chances of obtaining a license. Pay careful attention to each requirement and seek professional guidance to ensure you meet or exceed the necessary standards.

ANCILLARY CANNABIS BUSINESS TYPES

This section catalogs a variety of ancillary, non-plant-touching businesses critical to the cannabis industry. It spans consulting, technology, packaging, security, real estate, marketing, testing labs, equipment manufacturers, event planning, payment processing, legal, insurance, logistics, data analysis, education, waste management, genetics research, HVAC solutions, and more. These businesses support the ecosystem without directly dealing with the cannabis plant, offering services from regulatory compliance to operational efficiencies, underscoring the sector's diverse and integrated nature.

There are numerous ancillary or non-plant-touch cannabis businesses that provide essential services and products to the cannabis industry without directly handling the plant itself. Here are some examples:

Consulting: Companies that offer expertise in various aspects of the cannabis industry, including regulatory compliance, business strategy, and operational optimization.

Software and Technology: Development and sale of software solutions tailored for cannabis businesses, including point-of-sale systems, inventory management, compliance tracking, and data analytics.

Packaging and Labeling: Design and production of compliant packaging and labeling solutions for cannabis products.

Security Services: Providers of security systems, surveillance, and personnel to ensure the safety and compliance of cannabis businesses.

Real Estate: Companies specializing in leasing or selling real estate properties for cannabis cultivation, processing, and retail operations.

Marketing and Advertising: Marketing agencies that focus on cannabis businesses, offering services such as branding, digital marketing, and advertising.

Testing Laboratories: Independent laboratories that conduct testing on cannabis products to ensure quality, potency, and safety.

Packaging Equipment: Manufacturers and suppliers of machinery and equipment used for packaging cannabis products, including automated packaging systems.

Event Planning: Companies that organize cannabis-related events, conferences, and expos for industry networking and education.

Payment Processing: Financial technology companies providing secure and compliant payment processing solutions for cannabis transactions.

Legal Services: Law firms specializing in cannabis law, offering legal advice, regulatory compliance, and representation.

Insurance: Providers of insurance services tailored to the unique needs of cannabis businesses, including liability, property, and crop insurance.

Transportation and Logistics: Companies specializing in the transportation and distribution of cannabis products, ensuring compliance with regulatory requirements.

Extraction Equipment: Manufacturers and suppliers of equipment used for cannabis extraction processes, including CO2 extraction machines.

Data and Analytics: Companies that collect and analyze data related to the cannabis industry, providing insights for business decision-making.

Education and Training: Organizations offering educational programs and training courses for individuals entering the cannabis industry.

Compliance Software: Development and sale of software solutions specifically designed to assist cannabis businesses in maintaining regulatory compliance, tracking changes in laws, and managing licensing requirements.

Waste Management: Companies providing waste disposal and recycling services tailored to the unique requirements of cannabis businesses.

Genetics and Breeding: Businesses focused on cannabis genetics research and breeding programs to develop new strains and optimize plant characteristics.

Laboratory Equipment: Manufacturers and suppliers of specialized laboratory equipment used in cannabis testing, research, and development.

HVAC Systems: Providers of heating, ventilation, and air conditioning (HVAC) systems designed for cannabis cultivation facilities to maintain optimal environmental conditions.

Training: Training programs and platforms that offer courses on various aspects of the cannabis industry, including compliance, safety, and customer service.

Sustainability Solutions: Companies focused on providing environmentally sustainable solutions for energy, water, and waste management within the cannabis industry.

Recruitment and Staffing: Agencies specializing in recruiting and staffing services for cannabis businesses, helping them find qualified personnel.

Networking and Events Platforms: Online platforms and event organizers that facilitate networking and collaboration within the cannabis industry.

Compliance Consulting: Consultants who specialize in guiding cannabis businesses through regulatory compliance, ensuring adherence to local and state laws.

Insurance Brokers: Professionals who specialize in helping cannabis businesses find suitable insurance coverage tailored to their specific needs.

Accounting and Financial Services: Accounting firms and financial service providers specializing in the unique financial requirements of cannabis businesses.

Lab Accreditation Services: Organizations that offer accreditation services for cannabis testing laboratories, ensuring adherence to quality standards.

Technology Incubators: Incubators and accelerators focused on supporting startups and entrepreneurs in the development of innovative technologies for the cannabis industry.

These non-plant-touch cannabis businesses play a crucial role in supporting the overall growth, efficiency, and compliance of the cannabis industry. It is essential for entrepreneurs to explore these ancillary services to find opportunities for collaboration and business development.

CANNABIS TAX CODES

This section provides an overview of key cannabis tax codes and DEA scheduling in the United States, including the impact of Internal Revenue Code Section 280E on business deductions, various state-imposed excise, sales, cultivation, and local taxes on cannabis products and businesses. It highlights the unique financial and regulatory landscape cannabis businesses navigate, emphasizing the importance of staying informed on current laws and consulting with legal professionals for compliance.

It is important to note that laws and regulations related to cannabis are subject to change, and it's advisable to consult with legal professionals or check official government sources for the most up-to-date information. Below is a general overview of common cannabis tax codes and DEA scheduling in the United States:

Internal Revenue Code Section 280E: Section 280E of the Internal Revenue Code disallows businesses that traffic in controlled substances, including cannabis, from deducting normal business expenses for income tax purposes. This results in higher effective tax rates for cannabis businesses compared to other industries.

Excise Taxes: Some states impose excise taxes on the sale of cannabis products. These taxes are typically calculated based on the product's weight or potency.

Sales Tax: States often apply standard sales taxes to retail sales of cannabis products. The rates can vary depending on the state and local jurisdiction.

Cultivation Taxes: Some states impose taxes on the cultivation of cannabis plants, either based on square footage of cultivation space or the weight of harvested plants.

Local Taxes: Local jurisdictions may impose additional taxes on cannabis businesses operating within their boundaries.

DEA SCHEDULING

The Drug Enforcement Administration (DEA) categorizes controlled substances into schedules based on their perceived medical value and potential for abuse. As of April 2024, cannabis has been reclassified from a Schedule I to a Schedule III controlled substance under the Controlled Substances Act (CSA).

Schedule I vs. Schedule III

Schedule I: Previously, cannabis was classified as a Schedule I substance, indicating it had a high potential for abuse, no accepted medical use, and a lack of accepted safety for use under medical supervision. This classification placed significant restrictions on research, banking, and business operations within the cannabis industry.

Schedule III: The new classification acknowledges the medical benefits of cannabis and reflects a lower potential for abuse compared to Schedule I substances. This reclassification is expected to facilitate research and ease some of the federal restrictions impacting the cannabis industry. Schedule III substances are still controlled but are subject to less stringent regulatory requirements than Schedule I substances.

Implications of Rescheduling

Research: The reclassification to Schedule III will open up more opportunities for scientific research into the medical benefits of cannabis, enabling better understanding and development of cannabis-based therapies.

Banking and Financial Services: While the rescheduling may improve access to banking services for cannabis businesses, challenges remain due to the ongoing federal restrictions. However, it is expected to reduce some of the financial risks associated with operating in the cannabis industry.

Taxation: The change to Schedule III may affect tax regulations, specifically IRS Code Section 280E, potentially allowing cannabis businesses to deduct ordinary business expenses, which could lower their overall tax burden.

State Legalization: Despite federal rescheduling, state-level legalization efforts and regulations will continue to play a crucial role. The rescheduling does not legalize state-level programs but aligns federal policy more closely with the reality of state-legal cannabis markets.

It is important to note that the legal landscape regarding cannabis is dynamic, and changes at the federal, state, and local levels may occur. Businesses and individuals involved in the cannabis industry should consult with legal professionals or relevant government agencies for the most current and accurate information regarding cannabis tax codes and DEA scheduling.

CANNABIS LICENSE TYPES

The types of cannabis licenses available vary by jurisdiction, as each state or country with legalized cannabis has its own regulations and licensing categories. Below are common types of cannabis licenses, including those related to consumption lounges and clubs:

Cultivation License: Permits the cultivation of cannabis plants. Subcategories may include indoor, outdoor, and greenhouse cultivation.

Nursery License: Allows the cultivation of cannabis plants for the purpose of selling clones or seeds to other licensed cultivators.

Processor License: Authorizes the processing of cannabis into various products, such as extracts, edibles, topicals, and more.

Distribution License: Permits the transportation and distribution of cannabis products from cultivators or processors to dispensaries.

Dispensary License: Allows the retail sale of cannabis products directly to consumers for medical and/or recreational use.

Delivery License: Authorizes the delivery of cannabis products directly to consumers' homes.

Testing Laboratory License: Permits laboratories to conduct testing and analysis of cannabis products to ensure quality, safety, and compliance.

Event Organizer License: Allows the organization of cannabis-related events, including festivals, competitions, and educational events.

Temporary Event License: Permits temporary cannabis sales and consumption at authorized events.

Microbusiness License: Combines multiple activities, such as cultivation, processing, and retail, into a single license for small-scale operators.

Consumption Lounge License: Permits the operation of venues where consumers can purchase and consume cannabis on-site. Also known as cannabis lounges or social use establishments.

Private Club License: Allows private clubs to facilitate cannabis consumption for members.

Research and Development License: Authorizes institutions to conduct research on cannabis for medical or scientific purposes.
Social Equity Licenses: Some jurisdictions implement social equity programs that provide licensing preferences to individuals or communities disproportionately affected by cannabis prohibition.

Temporary Event Licenses: Some jurisdictions issue temporary licenses for specific events, allowing cannabis sales and consumption for a limited duration.

NOTE: Always refer to the specific regulations of the jurisdiction in question, as the types of licenses and associated requirements can vary significantly. Additionally, licensing categories and regulations may evolve over time as the cannabis industry continues to develop.

INTERNATIONAL CANNABIS ASSOCIATIONS

This section highlights international cannabis associations dedicated to advancing research, education, and collaboration across the global cannabis industry. Covering a wide range of focuses from medical research and industrial hemp to policy reform and patient advocacy, these organizations play a pivotal role in shaping the future of cannabis. They offer resources for professionals, patients, and advocates, working towards a more informed and unified global cannabis landscape.

There are several international cannabis associations and organizations that operate on a global scale. These associations work to promote research, education, and collaboration within the cannabis industry. Keep in mind that the landscape of cannabis regulations and organizations may have evolved, so it is advisable to verify the current status of these associations. Here are some international cannabis associations:

International Cannabis and Cannabinoids Institute (ICCI):

Website: https://www.icci.science/

International Association for Cannabinoid Medicines (IACM):

Website: https://www.cannabis-med.org/

European Industrial Hemp Association (EIHA):

Website: https://eiha.org/

International Medical Cannabis Patient Coalition (IMCPC):

Website: http://imcpc.org/

United Nations Office on Drugs and Crime (UNODC) - Cannabis Unit:

Website: https://www.unodc.org/

International Cannabis Business Conference (ICBC):

Website: https://internationalcbc.com/

International Hemp Building Association (IHBA):

Website: https://internationalhempbuilding.org/

International Drug Policy Consortium (IDPC):

Website: https://idpc.net/

Global Cannabis Partnership (GCP):

Website: https://www.globalcannabispartnership.com/

International Cannabis and Hemp Expo (INTCHE):

Website: https://intche.org/

International Cannabis Bar Association (INCBA):

Website: https://www.canbar.org/

World Health Organization (WHO) - Expert Committee on Drug Dependence (ECDD):

Website: https://www.who.int/

NOTE: These organizations cover various aspects of the cannabis industry, including medical research, industrial hemp, patient advocacy, business conferences, and drug policy. For the most accurate and current information, it is recommended to visit the official websites of these organizations. Additionally, new associations may have emerged, and the status of existing ones may have changed.

CANNABIS-RELATED TRADE SHOWS AND FESTIVALS

This section outlines prominent cannabis-related trade shows and festivals, serving as platforms for industry networking, education, and product showcasing. Events vary by location and adhere to local regulations, offering diverse opportunities for industry engagement. Attendees are advised to consult official event websites for the latest information on schedules and compliance with local laws.

Cannabis-related trade shows and festivals provide opportunities for networking, education, and showcasing products and services within the industry. The availability of events may vary based on location and regulations. Here are some notable cannabis-related tradeshows and festivals that were recognized. Keep in mind that event details and schedules may change, so it is recommended to check the official event websites for the most up-to-date information:

MJBizCon:

Website: https://mjbizconference.com/

Cannabis Cup:

Website: https://www.cannabiscup.com/

Cannabis Business Summit & Expo:

Website: https://www.cannabisbusinesssummit.com/

Hempfest:

Website: https://www.hempfest.org/

Spannabis:

Website: https://spannabis.com/

Hall of Flowers:

Website: https://www.hallofflowers.com/

CannaTech:

Website: https://www.canna-tech.co/

New West Summit:

Website: https://newwestsummit.com/

Emerald Cup:

Website: https://theemeraldcup.com/

Cannabis World Congress & Business Exposition (CWCBExpo):

Website: https://www.cwcbexpo.com/

Cannabis Science Conference:

Website: https://www.cannabisscienceconference.com/

CannX - Cannabis Medical Conference:

Website: https://www.cannx.org/

Cannabis Drinks Expo:

Website: https://cannabisdrinksexpo.com/

Cannabis Wedding Expo:

Website: https://www.cannabisweddingexpo.com/

Cannabis Liberation Day:

Website: https://www.cannabisliberationday.org/

Benzinga Cannabis Capital Conference:

Website: https://www.benzinga.com/events/cannabis-conference/

CANEXEC Toronto:

Website: https://canexecsummit.com/

NOTE: Before planning to attend any event, make sure to check the current status, dates, and details on the official event website. Additionally, considering the evolving nature of cannabis regulations, it is essential to verify compliance with local laws and restrictions regarding cannabis-related events.

VIABLE LIST OF FUNDING TYPES

This section provides a comprehensive list of funding options for cannabis startups, highlighting the diversity of financial sources available despite the unique challenges posed by the legal and regulatory environments of the cannabis industry. It underscores the importance of consulting with legal and financial experts to navigate these complexities effectively.

Here is a list of viable funding options for cannabis startups. Keep in mind that the availability of these options may vary based on legal and regulatory frameworks in different regions. Always consult legal and financial professionals for guidance specific to your location.

Private Investors: High-net-worth individuals, angel investors, and family offices may be willing to invest in promising cannabis startups.

Venture Capital (VC) Firms: Specialized cannabis-focused venture capital firms may provide funding to startups in the cannabis industry.

Equity Crowdfunding: Platforms like SeedInvest and Crowdcube allow businesses to raise funds by offering equity to a large number of small investors.

Debt Financing: Traditional bank loans or lines of credit, if available, can provide working capital. However, cannabis businesses may face challenges due to federal restrictions.

Strategic Partnerships: Form partnerships with established companies in related industries, such as pharmaceuticals or wellness, to access funding and industry expertise.

Grants and Competitions: Explore grants and competitions specifically designed for cannabis startups. Organizations like CanopyBoulder and The Arcview Group sometimes offer funding opportunities.

Incubators and Accelerators: Join cannabis-focused incubators and accelerators that provide funding, mentorship, and resources to startups. Examples include Gateway and CanopyBoulder.

Community Lending: Some local credit unions or community banks may be open to providing loans to cannabis businesses, depending on regional regulations.

Government Grants and Programs: In some regions, government agencies may offer grants or subsidies to support the growth of the cannabis industry.

Private Equity Firms: Explore partnerships with private equity firms that specialize in the cannabis sector.

Revenue-Based Financing: Platforms like Clearco (formerly Clearbanc) offer revenue-based financing, where startups repay the funding based on a percentage of their revenue.

Convertible Notes: Issuing convertible notes allows startups to raise funds as a loan, with an option for investors to convert the debt into equity later.

Equipment Financing: Secure financing specifically for equipment needed in cultivation, processing, or retail operations.

Initial Coin Offerings (ICOs) or Token Sales: In regions where permissible, blockchain-based fundraising through ICOs or token sales may be an option.

Supplier and Vendor Financing: Negotiate favorable payment terms with suppliers or vendors to improve cash flow.

Cannabis-Specific Lenders: Some financial institutions specialize in lending to cannabis businesses. Explore options provided by institutions familiar with the industry.

Social Impact Investors: Investors focused on social impact may be interested in supporting cannabis startups, especially those promoting wellness and responsible use.

Strategic Investors from Related Industries: Seek investments from companies in related industries, such as pharmaceuticals, health and wellness, or technology.

Peer-to-Peer Lending: Platforms like Prosper or LendingClub offer peer-to-peer lending options that may be suitable for certain funding needs.

Non-Dilutive Financing: Explore non-dilutive options like grants, contests, or competitions that do not require giving up equity.

NOTE: Remember to conduct thorough due diligence on potential investors, comply with legal regulations, and seek professional advice to choose the funding options that align with your business goals and the regulatory environment in your region.

CANNABIS BUSINESS PLAN TEMPLATE

This section outlines a comprehensive business plan template for cannabis ventures, detailing sections from executive summaries to financial projections. It guides entrepreneurs through defining their business concept, analyzing the market, organizing management, planning products/ services, strategizing sales and marketing, requesting funding, ensuring regulatory compliance, assessing risks, and setting timelines. This template is designed to help cannabis businesses articulate their vision, strategy, and operational plans, emphasizing the importance of adapting to local regulations and securing expert advice.

Executive Summary:

Business Name:

Founder(s) and Team:

Business Concept:

Mission Statement:

Vision:

Location:

Summary of Products/Services:

Financial Highlights:

Business Description:

> **Introduction to the Cannabis Industry:** Provide an overview of the cannabis industry and its current state.

Business Concept: Detail your business model, including the type of cannabis business (cultivation, processing, dispensary, etc.).

Legal Structure: Specify the legal structure of your business (LLC, corporation, etc.).

Market Analysis:

Industry Overview: Discuss trends, growth, and challenges in the cannabis industry.

Target Market: Identify your target customers and their demographics.

Competitor Analysis: Analyze competitors in your region.

SWOT Analysis: Outline your business' strengths, weaknesses, opportunities, and threats.

Organization and Management:

Founding Team: Introduce key team members, their roles, and expertise.

Organizational Structure: Provide an organizational chart.

Advisory Board: List any advisors or mentors.

Products/Services:

Product/Service Description: Detail your cannabis products or services.

Quality Control: Explain measures for quality control and compliance.

Pricing Strategy: Outline your pricing strategy.

Sales and Marketing:

Sales Strategy: Describe your sales approach.

Marketing Strategy: Outline your marketing plan, including online and offline strategies.

Brand Positioning: Define your brand positioning in the market.

Funding Request

Startup Costs: Provide an itemized list of startup expenses.

Funding Required: Specify the amount of funding required and how it will be used.

Use of Funds: Detail how the funds will be allocated.

Financial Projections:

Revenue Projections: Provide a detailed revenue forecast.

Expense Projections: Itemize your projected expenses.

Cash Flow Statement: Present a cash flow projection.

Regulatory Compliance:

Licensing Requirements: Detail the specific licenses needed for your cannabis business.

Compliance Plan: Outline your plan for staying compliant with local and state regulations.

Risk Analysis:

Identify Risks: Identify potential risks and challenges.

Mitigation Strategies: Provide strategies to mitigate identified risks.

Timeline:

Business Launch: Outline the timeline for launching your business.

Milestones: Set key milestones and deadlines.

Appendix:

> **Additional Information:** Include any additional documents, permits, or relevant information.

NOTE: Remember, this is a guide, and each section should be tailored to your specific business. Always stay informed about local regulations and adapt your business plan accordingly. Additionally, seek legal and financial advice to ensure compliance and sound financial planning.

STANDARD OPERATING PROCEDURE (SOP) TEMPLATE

This section provides a comprehensive template for creating Standard Operating Procedures (SOPs) tailored to the cannabis industry, detailing steps from purpose definition to execution, monitoring, and documentation. It includes guidelines for safety, compliance, training requirements, and approval processes, ensuring consistency, efficiency, and regulatory adherence in cannabis operations.

[Procedure Name]

Purpose: Clearly state the purpose of the procedure and its significance in the overall operation.

Scope: Define the boundaries and limits of the procedure. Specify the departments or individuals involved.

Responsibilities: Clearly outline the roles and responsibilities of each team member involved in the procedure.

Equipment and Materials: List all necessary equipment, tools, and materials required for the procedure.

Procedure:

> **Introduction:** Provide a brief overview of the procedure.

> **Preparation:** Detail the necessary preparations before executing the procedure.

> **Execution:** Step-by-step instructions for carrying out the procedure.

Monitoring: Specify any checkpoints or monitoring steps during the procedure.

Quality Control: Describe any quality control measures in place.

Troubleshooting: Provide solutions for common issues or challenges that may arise during the procedure.

Completion: Outline the steps to conclude the procedure.

Documentation: Specify any documentation or record-keeping requirements associated with the procedure.

Safety and Compliance: Detail safety measures and compliance requirements to ensure the well-being of personnel and adherence to regulations.

Review and Revision: Establish a schedule for periodic review and, if necessary, revision of the SOP.

Training: Identify any training requirements for personnel involved in the procedure.

References: Include any relevant documents, guidelines, or standards that support the procedure.

Approval: Provide space for signatures and dates to indicate approval from relevant stakeholders.

Revision History: Maintain a record of revisions made to the SOP, including dates and reasons for the changes.

Attachments: Include any supplementary materials or forms associated with the procedure.

Completed SOP Example:

Procedure Name: Cannabis Cultivation - Planting Seeds

Purpose:

To ensure consistent and proper planting of cannabis seeds for optimal germination and growth.

Scope:

Applies to the cultivation team responsible for planting seeds in the designated area.

Responsibilities:

Cultivation Manager: Oversees the entire planting process.

Cultivation Technicians: Responsible for executing the planting procedure.

Equipment and Materials:

Cannabis seeds

Germination trays

Growing medium

Watering cans

Procedure:

Introduction: This procedure outlines the steps for planting cannabis seeds to initiate the germination process.

Preparation: Ensure all equipment is clean and sterilized. Prepare germination trays with the appropriate growing medium.

Execution: Gently plant each seed at a depth of one inch. Water the trays evenly to ensure moisture penetration.

Monitoring: Check trays daily for signs of germination.

Quality Control: Ensure each seed is planted at the correct depth and receives adequate water.

Troubleshooting: If germination issues occur, assess watering levels, and adjust accordingly.

Completion: Once seeds have germinated, transfer seedlings to the next growth stage.

Documentation:

Record the number of seeds planted, germination rates, and any issues encountered.

Safety and Compliance:

Wear appropriate personal protective equipment (PPE) during the procedure.

Review and Revision:

Review this SOP annually or after any significant changes in cultivation practices.

Training:

New cultivation technicians must undergo training on this SOP.

References:

Cannabis Cultivation Guidelines (State Department of Agriculture)

Approval:

[Signature] Cultivation Manager [Date]

Revision History:

1.0 (Initial Version) - [Date]

1.1 (Revision) - [Date]

Attachments:

Germination Tray Setup Diagram

CANNABIS BUSINESS FINANCIAL PROJECTIONS TEMPLATE

This section introduces a financial projections template tailored for cannabis businesses, focusing on forecasting revenue, expenses, and cash flow. It includes calculations for cultivation and dispensary operations, offering a structured approach to estimate financial performance. Key elements cover revenue from harvests and sales, operational and administrative expenses, and cash flow analysis, alongside assumptions and key performance indicators like gross margin, net profit margin, and return on investment. This template is designed to help entrepreneurs plan financially, adapt to market conditions, and seek professional advice for accuracy and compliance.

Creating financial projections for a cannabis business involves forecasting income, expenses, and cash flow over a specific period. Below is a sample template for a simplified financial projection of a cannabis cultivation and dispensary business. Adjust the numbers and assumptions based on your specific business model, market conditions, and local regulations.

Revenue Projections:

Cultivation:

Projected Yield per Harvest: [XX] pounds

Number of Harvests per Year: [YY]

Estimated Sale Price per Pound: [$ZZZ]

Total Cultivation Revenue = [XX * YY * $ZZZ]

Dispensary:

Estimated Average Transaction Value: [$AAA]

Expected Number of Transactions per Day: [BBB]

Number of Operating Days per Year: [CCC]

Total Dispensary Revenue = [$AAA * BBB * CCC]

Total Revenue:

Total Annual Revenue = [Cultivation Revenue + Dispensary Revenue]

2. Expense Projections:

Cultivation:

Cost per Pound of Cannabis: [$XXX]

Total Cultivation Expenses = [XX * YY * $XXX]

Dispensary:

Operating Expenses (staff, rent, utilities, etc.): [$YYY]

General and Administrative:

Marketing and Advertising: [$ZZZ]

Regulatory Compliance: [$AAA]

Other Administrative Costs: [$BBB]

Total General and Administrative Expenses = [$ZZZ + $AAA + $BBB]

Total Expenses:

Total Annual Expenses = [Cultivation Expenses + Dispensary Expenses + General and Administrative Expenses]

Cash Flow Statement:

Net Cash Flow:

Net Cash Flow = [Total Annual Revenue - Total Annual Expenses]

Opening and Closing Cash Balance:

Opening Cash Balance = [$CCC]

Closing Cash Balance = [Opening Cash Balance + Net Cash Flow]

Assumptions:

Average Transaction Value Growth Rate:

Assumed growth rate for dispensary transactions.

Cultivation Yield Growth Rate:

Assumed growth rate for cultivation yield.

Expense Growth Rate:

Assumed growth rate for operating and administrative expenses.

Tax Rate:

Estimated tax rate on net income.

Key Performance Indicators (KPIs):

Gross Margin:

Gross Margin = [(Total Annual Revenue - Total Cultivation Expenses) / Total Annual Revenue] * 100

Net Profit Margin:

Net Profit Margin = [(Net Cash Flow / Total Annual Revenue) * 100]

Return on Investment (ROI):

ROI = [(Net Cash Flow / Total Startup Investment) * 100]

NOTE: This financial projection template provides a basis for estimating revenue, expenses, and cash flow for a cannabis business. It's crucial to regularly update and refine these projections based on actual performance and changing market conditions. Seek professional financial advice to ensure accuracy and compliance with accounting standards. Adjust assumptions as needed and conduct sensitivity analyses to understand potential impacts on financial outcomes.

CONCLUSION

As we conclude this comprehensive guide, it's essential to reflect on the journey we've embarked upon together. The cannabis industry is one of the most dynamic and rapidly evolving sectors, offering tremendous opportunities for those willing to invest the time, effort, and passion required to succeed. Whether you are a budding entrepreneur or an experienced professional seeking to pivot into this burgeoning field, the insights and strategies provided in this guide are designed to equip you with the knowledge and tools needed to thrive.

Embracing Change and Innovation

The cannabis industry is characterized by constant change, driven by evolving legal landscapes, scientific discoveries, and shifting consumer preferences. Staying informed and adaptable is crucial. Embrace innovation and be open to innovative ideas and technologies that can enhance your business operations and customer experience. Continuously educate yourself and your team, attend industry events, and network with other professionals to stay ahead of the curve.

Building a Resilient Business

Success in the cannabis industry requires resilience and a robust business strategy. From securing funding and navigating complex regulations to establishing a strong brand and fostering customer loyalty, each step in your journey will present unique challenges and opportunities. Use the frameworks and checklists provided in this guide to build a solid foundation for your business. Remember that resilience also involves learning from setbacks and continuously improving your processes and strategies.

Community and Social Responsibility

The cannabis industry offers a unique opportunity to make a positive impact on society. As you build your business, consider ways to give back to your community and promote social equity. Engage in sustainable practices, support local initiatives, and advocate for fair and inclusive policies. By doing so, you not only contribute to the betterment of society but also strengthen your brand's reputation and foster a loyal customer base.

Your Journey Ahead

As you venture into the world of cannabis entrepreneurship, keep in mind that this guide is just the beginning. The real journey begins now, and it is filled with endless possibilities. Leverage the resources, templates, and expert advice provided in this guide to navigate your path confidently. Surround yourself with a supportive network of mentors, partners, and peers who can offer guidance and encouragement.

Final Thoughts from the Author

Writing this guide has been a labor of love, inspired by my own experiences and the incredible potential I see in this industry. I am enthusiastic about helping others succeed and believe that by sharing knowledge and fostering a spirit of collaboration, we can all achieve wonderful things.

Thank you for allowing me to be a part of your entrepreneurial journey. I am excited to see the innovative and impactful businesses you will create. Remember, the key to success lies in persistence, adaptability, and a commitment to excellence. Stay curious, stay informed, and never stop striving for greatness.

Here's to your success in the cannabis industry!

FINAL RELECTIONS AND ACKOWLEGEMENTS

As we draw the curtain on this comprehensive guide through the *Cannabis Startup Success Guide*, it's with a profound sense of gratitude that we reflect on the invaluable contributions from each individual and organization that helped sculpt this guide into a beacon for those venturing into the vast and vibrant cannabis industry. My heartfelt appreciation goes out to staff at Canoja and RM Campbell Acquisitions, their added insights and expertise in cannabis technology and business acquisitions, respectively, have significantly enriched this guide. Their dedication and support have been instrumental in providing a well-rounded perspective on navigating the complexities of the cannabis market.

Embarking on a venture within the cannabis industry presents a unique blend of exhilaration and challenges. Through this guide, we aimed to equip you with the knowledge, strategies, and insights necessary to navigate the intricate landscape of cannabis entrepreneurship. As you step into this dynamic industry, remember that the keys to success lie in staying informed, adaptable, and compliant. The essence of the cannabis community is found in its commitment to collaboration, innovation, and responsible practices. Regardless of your role—be it in cultivation, processing, dispensary operations, or ancillary services—you are a crucial contributor to the ongoing evolution of the cannabis industry.

Looking ahead, this guide is but the first chapter in a series designed to illuminate the path to success in the cannabis sector. Future topics will delve deeper into each area covered, from licensing and legal frameworks to advanced marketing strategies, financial planning, and beyond. Each subsequent guide will build on the foundation laid here, introducing more nuanced insights and strategies tailored to the ever-evolving cannabis industry landscape.

As we venture forward, I must extend my deepest, most personal thanks to those who have been the cornerstone of my journey:

To my sons, for daily inspiring me to chase my dreams with energy and honesty. Your challenges encourage me to continually improve and be the best version of myself.

To my mother and my sister for your boundless love and support.

To my niece and nephew, for filling every moment with happiness.

To "My", for your steadfast support and faith in my dreams. You've created a nurturing space filled with peace, love, and joy, enabling me to be creative, feel inspired, focused, and cherished.

To all my friends and family across Georgia, Pennsylvania, Florida, New York, Maryland, California, and Jamaica, W.I., you know who you are.

Finally, and importantly, my canine companions, they deserve recognition for their instinctive ability to provide com fort during moments of stress and feeling overwhelmed. Their timely presence and calming influence by my side have been invaluable.

Thank you all for the roles you've played, no matter how large or small, in shaping my journey. Your support has been a beacon of light in the pursuit of my aspirations.

GLOSSARY OF TERMS

Cannabinoids: Chemical compounds found in cannabis plants that interact with the body's endocannabinoid system, affecting various physiological processes.

Canoja (Can-Oja): Cannabis Marketplace Platform

COGS (Cost of Goods Sold): Direct costs attributable to the production of the products sold by a company, including materials and labor.

Cultivation: The process of growing cannabis plants, which can vary in technique and setting (e.g., indoor, outdoor, greenhouse).

Dispensary: A retail store where cannabis products are sold legally to consumers for medical or recreational use.

Endocannabinoid System: A complex cell-signaling system identified in the early 1990s by researchers exploring THC, a well-known cannabinoid. It plays a role in regulating a range of functions and processes, including sleep, mood, appetite, memory, and reproduction and fertility.

Federal Prohibition: The ban or prohibition of cannabis under federal law in the United States, despite legalization in many states for medical or recreational use.

Hydroponics: A method of growing plants without soil, using mineral nutrient solutions in an aqueous solvent.

Indica and Sativa: Two primary species of the cannabis plant, each said to offer different effects and benefits. Indica is often associated with a more relaxing effect, while Sativa is said to be more energizing.

Licensing Requirements: Legal requirements and processes that cannabis businesses must follow to obtain permission to operate legally within a jurisdiction.

Section 280E: A provision of the U.S. Internal Revenue Code that disallows most business deductions for enterprises trafficking in controlled substances, including cannabis, as per federal law.

SOP (Standard Operating Procedure): A set of step-by-step instructions compiled by an organization to help workers conduct complex routine operations, aiming to achieve efficiency, quality output, and uniformity of performance.

Strains: Genetic variants or subspecies of the cannabis plant, bred to produce distinct effects, flavors, and aromas.

THC (Tetrahydrocannabinol): The main psychoactive compound in cannabis, responsible for the high sensation.

Topicals: Cannabis-infused lotions, balms, and oils that are absorbed through the skin for localized relief of pain, soreness, and inflammation.

Vertical Integration: A business model where a single company controls multiple stages of production typically involved in various stages of the cannabis supply chain, from cultivation to retail.

Zoning Laws: Regulations governing the use of land and the buildings on it, including specifications of where commercial enterprises like cannabis businesses can be located.